Engaging God's Word

Colossians

Engage Bible Studies

Tools That Transform

Engage Bible Studies

an imprint of

 COMMUNITY BIBLE STUDY

Engaging God's Word: Colossians
Copyright © 2013 by Community Bible Study. All rights reserved.
ISBN 978-1-62194-002-9

Published by Community Bible Study
790 Stout Road
Colorado Springs, CO
1-800-826-4181
www.communitybiblestudy.org

Unless otherwise noted, all Scriptures are taken from the *Holy Bible, English Standard Version*®, ESV®. Copyright ©2001 by Crossway, a publishing ministry of Good News Publishers. Used by permission. All rights reserved worldwide.

All rights reserved. No part of this publication may be reproduced, stored in a retrieval system, or transmitted in any form or by any means—electronic, mechanical, photocopy, recording, or any other—without prior written permission of Community Bible Study.

Printed in the United States of America.

Contents

Introduction

Welcome to the life-changing adventure of engaging with God's Word!
Whether this is the first time you've opened a Bible or you've studied
the Scriptures all your life, good things are in store for you. Studying
the Bible is unlike any other kind of study you have ever done. That's
because the Word of God is *"living and active"* (Hebrews 4:12) and
transcends time and cultures. The earth and heavens as we know them
will one day pass away, but God's Word never will (Mark 13:31). It's
as relevant to your life today as it was to the people who wrote it down
centuries ago. And the fact that God's Word is living and active means
that reading God's Word is always meant to be a personal experience.
God's Word is not just dead words on a page—it is page after page
of living, powerful words—so get ready, because the time you spend
studying the Bible in this *Engaging God's Word* course will be life-
transforming!

Why Study the Bible?

Some Christians read the Bible because they know they're supposed to.
It's a good thing to do, and God expects it. And all that's true! However,
there are many additional reasons to study God's Word. Here are just
some of them.

We get to know God through His Word. Our God is a relational God
who knows us and wants us to know Him. The Scriptures, which He
authored, reveal much about Him: how He thinks and feels, what His
purposes are, what He thinks about us, how He views the world He
made, what He has planned for the future. The Bible shows us God's
many attributes—His kindness, goodness, justice, love, faithfulness,
mercy, compassion, creativity, redemption, sovereignty, and so on. As
we get to know Him through His Word, we come to love and trust Him.

God speaks to us through His Word. One of the primary ways God speaks to us is through His written Word. Don't be surprised if, as you read the Bible, certain parts nearly jump off the page at you, almost as if they'd been written with you in mind. God is the Author of this incredible book, so that's not just possible, it's likely! Whether it is to find comfort, warning, correction, teaching, or guidance, always approach God's Word with your spiritual ears open (Isaiah 55:3) because God, your loving heavenly Father, has things He wants to say to you.

God's Word brings life. Just about everyone wants to learn the secret to "the good life." And the good news is, that secret is found in God's Word. Don't think of the Bible as a bunch of rules. Viewing it with that mindset is a distortion. God gave us His Word because as our Creator and the Creator of the universe, He alone knows how life was meant to work. He knows that love makes us happier than hate, that generosity brings more joy than greed, and that integrity allows us to rest more peacefully at night than deception does. God's ways are not always "easiest" but they are the way to life. As the Psalmist says, *"If Your law had not been my delight, I would have perished in my affliction. I will never forget Your precepts, for by them You have given me life"* (Psalm 119:92-93).

God's Word offers stability in an unstable world. Truth is an ever-changing negotiable for many people in our culture today. But building your life on constantly changing "truth" is like building your house on shifting sand. God's Word, like God Himself, never changes. What He says was true yesterday, is true today, and will still be true a billion years from now. Jesus said, *"Everyone then who hears these words of Mine and does them will be like a wise man who built his house on the rock"* (Matthew 7:24).

God's Word helps us to pray effectively. When we read God's Word and get to know what He is really like, we understand better how to pray. God answers prayers that are according to His will. We discover His will by reading the Bible. First John 5:14-15 tells us that *"this is the confidence that we have toward Him, that if we ask anything according to His will He hears us. And if we know that He hears us in whatever we ask, we know that we have the requests that we have asked of Him."*

How to Get the Most out of *Engaging God's Word*

Each *Engaging God's Word* study contains key elements that have been carefully designed to help you get the most out of your time in God's Word. Slightly modified for your study-at-home success, this approach is very similar to the tried-and-proven Bible study method that Community Bible Study has used with thousands of men, women, and children across the United States and around the world for nearly 40 years. There are some basic things you can expect to find in each course in this series.

❖ Lesson 1 provides an overview of the Bible book (or books) you will study and questions to help you focus, anticipate, and pray about what you will be learning.

❖ Every lesson contains questions to answer on your own, commentary that reviews and clarifies the passage, and three special sections called "Apply what you have learned," "Think about" and "Personalize this lesson."

❖ Some lessons contain memory verse suggestions.

Whether you plan to use *Engaging God's Word* on your own or with a group, here are some suggestions that will help you enjoy and receive the most benefit from your study.

Spread out each lesson over several days. Your *Engaging God's Word* lessons were designed to take a week to complete. Spreading out your study rather than doing it all at once allows time for the things God is teaching you to sink in and for you to practice applying them.

Pray each time you read God's Word. The Bible is a book unlike any other because God Himself inspired it. The same Spirit who inspired the human authors who wrote it will help you to understand and apply it if you ask Him to. So make it a practice to ask Him to make His Word come alive to you every time you read it.

Read the whole passage covered in the lesson. Before plunging into the questions, take time to read the specific chapter or verses that will be covered in that lesson. Doing this will give you important context for the whole lesson. Reading the Bible in context is an important principle in interpreting it accurately.

Begin learning the memory verse. Learning Scripture by heart requires discipline, but the rewards far outweigh the effort. Memorizing a verse allows you to recall it whenever you need it—for personal encouragement and direction, or to share with someone else. Consider writing the verse on a sticky note or index card that you can post where you will see it often or carry with you to review during the day. Reading and re-reading the verse often—out loud when possible—is a simple way to commit it to memory.

Re-read the passage for each section of questions. Each lesson is divided into sections so that you study one small part of Scripture at a time. Before attempting to answer the questions, review the verses that the questions will cover.

Answer the questions without consulting the Commentary or other reference materials. There is great joy in having the Holy Spirit teach you God's Word on your own, without the help of outside resources. Don't cheat yourself of the delight of discovery by reading the Commentary prematurely. Wait until after you've completed the lesson.

Repeat the process for all the question sections.

Prayerfully consider the "Apply what you have learned," marked with the ⚲ push pin symbol. The vision of Community Bible Study is not to just gain knowledge about the Bible, but to be transformed by it. For this reason, each set of questions closes with a section that encourages you to apply what you are learning. Usually this section involves action—something for you to do. As you practice these suggestions, your life will change.

Read the Commentary. *Engaging God's Word* commentaries are written by theologians whose goal is to help you understand the context of what you are studying as it relates to the rest of Scripture, God's character, and what the passage means for your life. Of necessity, the commentaries include the author's interpretations. While interesting and helpful, keep in mind that the Commentary is simply one person's understanding of what these passages mean. Other godly men and women have views that are also worth considering.

Pause to contemplate each "Think about" section, marked with the notepad symbol. These features, embedded in the Commentary, offer a place to pause and consider some of the principles being brought out by the text. They provide excellent ideas to journal about or to discuss with other believers, especially those doing the study with you.

Jot down insights or prayer points from the "Personalize this lesson" marked with the ☑ check box symbol. While the "Apply what you have learned" section focuses on doing, the "Personalize this lesson" section focuses on becoming. Spiritual transformation is not just about doing right things and refraining from doing wrong things—it is about changing from the inside out. To be transformed means letting God change our hearts so that our attitudes, emotions, desires, reactions, and goals are increasingly like Jesus'. Often this section will discuss something that you cannot do in your own strength—so your response will usually be something to pray about. Remember that becoming more Christ-like is not just a matter of trying harder—it requires God's empowerment.

Jesus Is Lord of All

In this Bible study you will explore an idea of profound importance to our faith—the idea of Jesus Christ's pre-eminence. The short book of Colossians declares that Christ is the source of everything and that He has absolute authority and superiority over everything—whether visible or invisible, past, present, or future—everything!

- ❖ He is Lord over creation.

- ❖ He is Lord over angels, demons, and all spiritual powers.

- ❖ He is Lord over wisdom and knowledge, and greater than all human philosophy.

- ❖ He delivered men and women from the domain of darkness and brought them into His kingdom.

- ❖ He indwells believers renewing them after the image of their Creator.

- ❖ He empowers believers to live in loving relationship with each other.

1. Are any of the truths in the list you just read new to you? Which one(s)?

_____

_____

_____

_____

2. Which one intrigues you most? Why?

_____

_____

3. Which one seems most relevant to your life right now? Why?

_____

_____

4. As we study God's Word, our goal is to be transformed by it. As you think about the truths you will be studying in this course, which one seems most important for your spiritual growth right now?

_____

_____

_____

If you are doing this study with a group, take time to pray for one another about your answers to question 4. Ask God to reveal truth to you as you study about this and even more importantly, to make you more like Jesus as a result. If you are studying by yourself, write your prayer in the blank space below.

Jesus Is Lord of All

Colossians was written to correct false teachings that were infiltrating the church in Colossae and threatening to weaken or destroy the believers' faith in the Lordship and sufficiency of Jesus Christ. The letter is particularly well suited for ministry to believers during any period when error is seeping into the church through the thinking or teaching of pastors, teachers, or well-meaning lay men and women.

Background

The little city of Colossae was on its way to becoming a ghost town when Paul wrote to the young church there. Not many years before, Colossae, in present-day south-central Turkey, had been a thriving center of commerce. But at the time of Paul's writing, Laodicea and Hierapolis were leaving Colossae in the commercial dust. Colossae never recovered its former glory and power.

For more than 200 years, Colossae hosted a large Jewish population. The city's commercial opportunities had attracted many who sought to escape the depressed economy left in the wake of the Maccabean wars in Israel. As these Jews settled in the new land, they compromised with Hellenistic thought. These transplanted Jews left behind much of the tradition that gave definition to life in Israel.

Paganism flourished in Colossae. The area was known for its participation in various Greek mystery religions with their bizarre and immoral practices. Gnosticism was capturing the minds of the Colossians. All of this was already affecting the early church in Colossae. The deterioration of their belief system was producing degeneration of their lifestyle.

Think about how the culture of a person's community can affect their spiritual life—for good, or for ill. How does the community in which you live impact your walk with God? Talk to God about it.

The Gnostics taught that matter was evil and spirit was good. This teaching necessitated a belief that God had no direct involvement in creating this wicked world. In practice, it also resulted in either ascetic denial of natural physical desires or wanton indulgence of them. But there is an even greater theological significance to separating matter and spirit: If Gnosticism were true, the flesh and spirit could not be combined in Jesus, the unique God/man. It would be impossible for such a man to be the Savior, for He would have flesh and thus a sinful nature. So the Gnostics taught that Jesus was a distant cousin of God, by no means equal to God.

Gnostics taught that Jesus became divine at His baptism, and then the nature of God left Him at His crucifixion, when He cried out, *"It is finished"* (John 19:30). Special insights into religious "truth" were given to the special few who were the "knowing ones"—hence the name *Gnostics*, from the Greek word *gnosis*, meaning *to know*.

Christianity in Colossae was at a crossroads. The people faced two options: follow Gnosticism's belief in a distant, disinterested deity, or follow Christianity, which offered personal relationship with a loving God who is intimately involved with His creation and His people.

The book of Colossians forms Paul's most eloquent statement concerning the person and work of Jesus Christ. He is introduced as the fullness of the Godhead in physical form—the Son of God, who is truly God and truly man, yet absolutely without sin.

It seems likely that Epaphras was serving as pastor of the Colossian church when the pressures of Judaic legalism with its rules and ceremonies, and pagan mysticism with its astrology, horoscopes, and angel worship, prompted him to go to Paul for guidance and help.

Date of Writing

There is some question as to the exact date and place from which Paul wrote Colossians. The traditional view holds that the letter was written between AD 60–62, during Paul's house arrest in Rome as he waited for his case to come before the emperor (Acts 28). A second view suggests that Paul wrote the book from Ephesus between AD 54–57. This view is based on the fact that it would have been easy and natural for Epaphras to travel the 80 miles between Colossae and Ephesus to enlist Paul's help.

Author

Paul is the primary author of Colossians, although he credits Timothy as co-author. Paul introduces himself simply as an apostle of Jesus Christ.

Paul was incredibly intelligent. He wrote 13 of the 27 New Testament books; some scholars also credit him with authoring Hebrews. But Paul had more than the mind of a great theologian. He had the heart of a great pastor. Furthermore, his background combined the three major racial and cultural groups of his day. Paul was:

- ❖ born of Jewish parents and trained under the respected rabbi Gamaliel
- ❖ a Roman citizen from birth by inheritance from his father
- ❖ born in Tarsus, a center of Greek culture and home to a great university

God sovereignly chose and uniquely qualified Paul to take the gospel to the Gentiles. Timothy, his son in the faith, often traveled and ministered with him. Together they produced a book exhorting believers to stand firm in their faith, to live lives worthy of the Lord, and to please Him in every way.

Personalize this lesson.

To counter the false doctrine being spread through the Colossian church, Paul centered his letter to them on truth. His approach was caring and empathetic. He reminded the Colossians of God's faithfulness to them in the past. He assured them of his unceasing prayer on their behalf. But above all, he fixed their gaze on Christ's preeminence and power, far surpassing the spurious insight of the deceptive philosophies besieging the young church. Paul desired that they would *know* Christ closely enough to escape the delusion and captivity of false teachings. He wrote a victorious testament to Jesus' resurrection and supremacy, encouraging the Colossians with the knowledge that this same power was alive within their hearts, equipping them to conquer temptation and combat deception. Paul's approach can serve as a model for us today when we face our own times of confusion and disillusionment. As Paul did, we can focus on knowing truth and knowing Christ, which will help us detect false doctrine when it comes our way.

Lesson 2

Christ's People
Colossians 1:1-14

Memorize God's Word: Colossians 1:13-14.

❖ Colossians 1:1-2a—Introductions

1. Read this short book in one sitting if at all possible. It should not take more than 20 minutes. Record one idea Paul writes of in this book that you want to think about more in depth, and the reason you chose it.

    _____

    _____

2. How does Paul describe himself in verse 1?

    _____

    _____

3. Why do you think Paul chooses to describe himself the way he does?

    _____

    _____

4. Paul calls the Colossian believers *"saints,"* which some Bible translations render as *"God's holy people"* (NIV). According to 1 Peter 1:14-23, what qualifies a person to be called *holy*?

    _____

    _____

❖ Colossians 1:2b-5—A Saint's Calling

5. The Bible often speaks of *grace*. One definition of grace describes it as *the covenant love of God*; another defines it as *undeserved, unearned favor with God*. Record what the following passages teach about the gracious way God works with us.

   a. Luke 15:11-24 _____

   _____

   _____

   b. Ephesians 2:8-10 _____

   _____

   _____

6. *Faith* is both a belief and an action. Read the examples of faith in Mark 10:46-52 and Luke 7:36-50, and write your own definition of faith.

   _____

   _____

❖ Colossians 1:6-8—A Saint's Contribution

7. Verse 6 tells us that the gospel is producing fruit all over the world. List some examples of how the gospel has produced fruit in

   a. various faraway places _____

   _____

   _____

   b. your own life _____

   _____

   _____

8. From verses 7-8, comment on the way the news of God's love was being spread.

   _____

   _____

9. What do you glean from Epaphras's example about the importance of teaching biblical truth as an essential part of faithful ministry? (Read also Romans 10:11-14.)

    _____

    _____

❖ Colossians 1:9-12—God's Will for a Saint

10. What did Paul constantly ask God to do for the Colossian Christians?

    _____

    _____

11. Why did Paul pray the way he did?

    _____

    _____

12. How would you describe a life that is *"worthy of the Lord"*?

    _____

    _____

13. What source of power is available to Christians? (See also Philippians 4:13.)

    _____

    _____

14. What is God's purpose for making His power available to us, according to Colossians 1:11?

    _____

    _____

15. What qualifies a person for an inheritance in God's kingdom? (See also Ephesians 1:3-14.)

    _____

    _____

    _____

❖ Colossians 1:13-14—A Saint's Inheritance

16. What did God rescue you from when you began to follow Christ? (See also Ephesians 6:11-17.) Please give a general biblical answer and a personal answer.

_____

_____

_____

_____

17. If jewelry taken to a pawn shop is not redeemed by its owner, it becomes the shop's property. Using this analogy, describe what happened to you when Christ redeemed you by His blood.

_____

_____

_____

18. How would you describe what takes place when God forgives our sins? (See also Psalms 32:1-5; 51:7-10; 103:12.)

_____

_____

_____

_____

Apply what you have learned. How does Paul's prayer (1:3-14) compare to the prayers you pray for those you love and thank God for? What do you learn that could make your prayers more meaningful and effective?

Christ's People
Colossians 1:1-14

The Addressees

Paul begins his letter by telling the believers at Colossae that they are *"saints and faithful brothers in Christ"* (Colossians 1:2). Yet the concept of being a saint seems unfamiliar and uncomfortable to most people today. The Greek word translated *saint* in the ESV is the word also used for *holy*. In the adjective form, it means *clean*. In the Greek religion, it was used of sacred items in a temple that were reserved for use by the gods. So when Paul calls the Colossians *holy* or *saints*, he is calling them *vessels cleaned and set apart for God's pleasure and personal use*.

Paul unites two greetings that were familiar in the 1ˢᵗ century, *grace* and *peace*. In essence he is saying, "May God bless you far beyond what you deserve and give you peace—not dependent on your circumstances— that you can receive only from Him."

God desires that all His people experience *faith*, *love*, and *hope*. Notice the progression: *faith* in Christ brings about *love*, which produces *hope*. When we have *faith* in Christ, we are able to show the *love* of Christ. Seeing this type of love developed in our lives is living proof that God is at work in us—and confirms our *hope* of heaven.

Perhaps the most often discussed yet misunderstood aspect of the Christian life is prayer. *Prayer is a conversation between a person and God.* Effective praying involves listening as well as speaking. Speaking involves praise, petition, and talking with God. Praise is recounting God's attributes and actions and thanking Him for His great accomplishments on our behalf. General petition (*"Your will be done,"* Matthew 6:10) and specific petition (*"Give us this day our daily bread,"* 6:11) are examples of prayer for God's specific provision or intervention. The Bible repeatedly urges constant communication with God; e.g., *"Pray without ceasing"* and *"Give thanks in all circumstances"* (1 Thessalonians 5:18).

Listening involves tuning into the Holy Spirit's voice. We can do this as we read Scripture, listening to God's heart, rather than merely learning facts about Him. As we meditate on His Words and ways, He may reveal things about His purposes that apply to our individual situations. We can also listen to Him as we ponder nature, or the circumstances and events around us. We may notice His subtle promptings as we go about our day. We can make a habit of bringing our questions and decisions to Him, then asking Him to lead us into truth and life. He promises to guide our paths if we will trust in Him with all our hearts and not lean on our own understanding (Proverbs 3:5-6).

Living According to God's Will

Paul prays that the Colossians might perceive and have the power to perform God's will and that God may help them to *"walk in a manner worthy of the Lord, fully pleasing to Him"* (Colossians 1:10).

To do this, we need *knowledge, understanding,* and *wisdom* (1:9-10). Although the words are sometimes used as synonyms, they are distinct. *Knowledge* refers to *facts* required for right living. *Understanding* involves the *motivation* for right living. *Wisdom* is about applying what we know, the *skill* for right living. A growing knowledge of God enables us to bear fruit in every good work. He delights in strengthening us for this purpose through *"His glorious might"* (1:11).

Think about Philippians 4:13: *"I can do all things through* [Christ]." This doesn't mean we can do anything we desire, but that anything He wants us to do can be done through the power of Christ. If we must get over a great obstacle or deal with a great hurt, Christ promises to be there with us and to help us.

Endurance, one of the character traits that God's power gives, is *the ability to continue to do what is necessary, to refuse to give up or quit.* *Patience,* a more passive trait that usually is tested by difficult people or circumstances, is *the ability to go on with grace and peace when you cannot alter a situation.* Jesus *"for the joy that was set before Him endured the cross"* and *"endured from sinners such hostility against Himself"* (Hebrews 12:2-3). He was patient with His disciples (Luke 22:24-27, 31-34; John 14:5-9) when they seemed confused or obtuse.

Joy is from the Greek word *chara*, meaning *gladness*. In today's world, we have a tendency to believe that if we can escape hardship, then we will have joy. But the Bible indicates that the opposite is true. Joy is different from happiness. Joy does not depend on people or circumstances. It depends entirely on the fact that Christ lives in us and is able to bring goodness and redemption out of our trials and troubles.

Colossians 1:12 says that *"the Father ... has qualified you to share in the inheritance of the saints in light."* This is one of the most amazing statements in all of Scripture because it underscores once again that salvation is not the result of man's clamoring after God, but is a gift freely given by God Himself.

Why should we want to *"walk in a manner worthy of the Lord, fully pleasing to Him"* (1:10)? The motivation is what He has done for us—our salvation. We do not try to please Him to earn our salvation. Instead, we respond to His gracious, undeserved gift to us. Consider what the Lord did: He delivered us from darkness, redeemed us, and forgave us (1:13, 14).

Some people might object, "Forgave us of what? We're basically good people. What does God find so offensive that requires Him to forgive us before He can welcome us into His family?"

If we're honest, even the best of us must admit that we have attitudes and behaviors that hurt ourselves and others, not to mention God. Fear, jealousy, anger, prejudice, hatred, ambition, impatience, selfishness, greed, and lust destroy us and degrade others. We need His rescue, redemption, and forgiveness! So we joyfully give thanks to the Father, who has qualified us to share in His good gifts.

Personalize this lesson.

☑ In his prayer for the Colossian believers, Paul's opening statement is that he always thanks God for them because he has heard of their faith in Jesus and their love for the other believers. Do you know someone who encourages you by their faith in Jesus and their love for other believers? Do you bring that same joy to those who know you? Thank God for the ways you have grown in faith and love over the time you have walked with Jesus. Ask Him for grace to grow even more in these beautiful qualities.

Christ's Identity
Colossians 1:15-2:7

Memorize God's Word: Colossians 1:19-20.

❖ Colossians 1:15-20—Christ Preeminent

1. Some people say that Jesus was godly but not the same as God. What do verses 15-20 state about Jesus that could be true only of God?

    _____

    _____

    _____

2. Record what the following references tell you about Jesus.

    a. Psalm 2:7 _____

    _____

    b. Isaiah 9:6 _____

    _____

    c. John 3:16 _____

    _____

3. What role did Christ play in creation? (See also John 1:1-4 and Hebrews 1:2-3.)

    _____

    _____

    _____

❖ Colossians 1:20-23—Christ, the Reconciler

4. Why was it necessary for Christ to die physically on the cross? (See also Romans 5:6-8; Hebrews 9:22.)

5. What caused the enmity between God and the human race? (See also Romans 1:18-32.)

6. From verse 21 and 2 Corinthians 4:1-4, where does the enmity start?

7. How would you summarize in your own words the gospel that Paul declares?

❖ Colossians 1:24-2:2—Love for God's People

8. Why is Paul willing to suffer for Christ?

9. What is the *"mystery"* referred to here?

10. a. Review Colossians 1:10-12 and record the result of being empowered by God.

b.   What other use of God's energy is referred to in verse 29?

_____

_____

11. What is the goal of evangelism, according to verse 28?

_____

_____

❖ Colossians 2:2b-4—Love for God's Word

12. In what ways is God's wisdom superior to man's wisdom? (See also 1 Corinthians 1:18-31.)

_____

_____

_____

13. Read Psalm 119:9-16, 97-105.

a.   What additional information does the psalmist give about God's wisdom as revealed in His Word?

_____

_____

_____

b.   What is our best protection against heretical doctrines and false teachers?

_____

_____

❖ Colossians 2:5-7—Maturing in Faith

14. It is puzzling to see people profess their faith but never see any evidence of a changed life. What will help to produce fruit in a new Christian's life, according to verses 6-7?

_____

_____

15. List the marks of Christian maturity mentioned in the following verses:

    a.   Colossians 2:5-6 _____

        _____

        _____

    b.   Ephesians 5:15-21 _____

        _____

        _____

    c.   What marks of Christian maturity are found in
        1 Thessalonians 5:14-22?

        _____

        _____

        _____

        _____

Apply what you have learned. Paul *struggles* for other believers, that their hearts may be encouraged, that they may be knit together in love, that they have full assurance of understanding and knowledge of Christ, and that they not be deluded by plausible—but false—arguments. Consider what it means to have the spiritual welfare of another at heart. Who do you care about spiritually? What might it look like for you to struggle for them spiritually?

Christ's Identity
Colossians 1:15-2:7

Image of God

When God's Son was born into our world, all heaven joined with Jesus' earthly parents in celebration. The Old Testament prophet Isaiah predicted the excitement: *"To us a child is born!"* (Isaiah 9:6).

But the excitement is not just in the birth of *a* child; it is in the birth of *this* child. This child who was born is truly human. This Son who was given is truly divine. Jesus Christ is both God and man.

The English word *image* in Colossians 1:15 comes from the Greek word *eikon*, meaning *reflection*. When we think of an image or reflection, we think of a one-dimensional image as in a mirror. But 1:19 gives us a three-dimensional view of the Son who was given: *"In Him all the fullness of God was pleased to dwell."*

Think about why many parents make videos of their children. Videos add the dimensions of sound and motion to the record of their children's development. Jesus added sound and motion to our picture of God. He even added flesh and bones. Everything we need to know about God can be known because Jesus came to make Him known. There's an important difference between knowing *about* Jesus and actually *knowing* Him—having a relationship with Him. If you're not sure of your relationship, talk to your pastor or a mature Christian friend.

"*By Him all things were created, in heaven and on earth, visible and invisible, whether thrones or dominions or rulers or authorities—all things were created through Him and for Him*" (Colossians 1:16). No one but an all-powerful, all-knowing God is sufficient in power and intelligence to account for the order, beauty, and majesty we see in the world around us. The Bible presents the child in the manger as the omnipotent, omniscient Creator. But He is more.

God breathed life into our planet. He created it and then took the responsibility for sustaining and preserving it. That necessitated His getting actively involved in saving it—and us—from the mess we humans have made of our world and our lives. People who have trusted Jesus to save them make up the church—His body—which He heads.

All the world's other religions attempt to show human beings how to reach God. But the message of the Bible is that God reached down to humans. People instinctively feel that they must make a peace offering to appease the God they have offended. But God Himself made a peace offering. In the life of Jesus, we learn that God loves us and in mercy longs to pardon and save us. Because God condemned our sin but then paid the penalty Himself, we have hope. God took the initiative to reconcile the world to Himself.

Paul does not state that Christ is *a* hope of glory. He states that Christ in you is *the* hope of glory. In an age characterized by pluralism, which values tolerance and accepts all ideas as having equal value, that is a controversial statement. The problem with such a philosophy lies in the nature of truth. If Christ's claims are true, there is *no other way* to God. Jesus Christ is the *Lord of glory* and our only *hope of glory*.

Truth these days is no longer defined objectively. For many, truth is whatever is "true for me" or "true for you." Such conventional wisdom says that everyone brings some part of the universal truth to the discussion of religion, so be tolerant, inclusive, and aim for synthesis.

To be intellectually honest, however, we must ask this question: Is there any objective way of determining whether or not there is a substantive difference between Christianity and the many other world religions and philosophies? The Bible insists that truth can be known; that Jesus Christ *is* Truth incarnate; that He can be known; and that He makes God known to us.

Claims Proven

The truth of Christianity rests on the claims of Jesus, and the claims of Jesus rest upon two pillars: *revelation* and *resurrection*.

Jesus' claim of deity causes many inquirers to stop short. But it cannot be disputed that Jesus claimed to be God. He said, *"I and the Father are one"* (John 10:30). His enemies accused Him of blasphemy because He claimed to be God (John 10:33). To authenticate His claim to deity, Jesus demonstrated divine power as He raised the dead, healed the sick, delivered the demonized, and controlled nature with His word. This is revelation.

Christ's resurrection is the essential second pillar for belief in His deity. Logic dictates that if Jesus had claimed to be equal with God (John 5:18) and was not, God easily could have left Jesus' lifeless body in the tomb and forcefully shown all who would follow Him the folly of their faith. *But He did not!* As He had predicted, Jesus *did* rise from the dead, vindicating His claims.

The miracle of Easter is central to Christianity—and troubling to those who reject Jesus' deity. English novelist H. G. Wells wrote: "Let's talk about the miracle of resurrection. If it is true, the [other miracles] are easily explained. If it is false, they don't matter." Simon Greenleaf, a 19th century legal scholar, wrote, "The resurrection is the most established fact in history."

Calling of Saints

In Colossians 1:28-2:7, Paul describes the character of a Christian and tells us that God expects much from us. What does it mean to be mature in Christ? It does not mean being sinless. It means we become all that God intended for us to be. In Colossians 2:1-7 Paul lists three evidences of maturity: love for God's people, full understanding, and strong faith.

Paul says believers have *"full assurance of understanding … of God's mystery"* (2:2), so they will not be deceived by faulty arguments about Christ's identity. The Word of God is our only reliable source for knowledge about Jesus and His salvation.

Personalize this lesson.

Read 2:7 again. What does it look like to walk with Jesus? To be rooted in Him? To be built up in Him? To be established in the faith? To abound in thanksgiving? Pick one of these areas in which you would like to grow. Talk to Jesus about it. Thank Him for His willingness to help you. Then consciously and specifically seek His help in this this week.

Christ's Supremacy
Colossians 2:8-23

Memorize God's Word: Colossians 2:8.

❖ Colossians 2:8-10—The Problem With Reason

1. Is the Christian faith opposed to all philosophy?

   _____

2. What two forces are behind empty, deceptive philosophy, according to verse 8?

   _____

   _____

3. Conversely, what is basic to good philosophy?

   _____

   _____

   _____

4. What essential Christian doctrine is affirmed in verse 9? (See also 1 John 2:22; 4:2.)

   _____

   _____

5. What do you understand it to mean that we *"have been filled in Him"* (Colossians 2:10)?

   _____

   _____

❖ Colossians 2:11-15—Rituals and Codes

6. What was the original significance of circumcision to Jews? (See Genesis 17:1-14.)

_____

_____

7. Read Deuteronomy 10:12-17 and Jeremiah 4:3-4. How had the meaning of circumcision changed?

_____

_____

8. What is the meaning of the circumcision described in Colossians? (See also Romans 2:28-29.)

_____

_____

9. List what Colossians 2:13-15 says God does for us at salvation.

_____

_____

10. What do you understand the phrase *"made alive together with Him"* (2:13) to mean?

_____

_____

11. What is the *"record of debt that stood against us"* that Christ canceled when He died on the cross? (See also Galatians 3:23-25.)

_____

_____

❖ Colossians 2:15—Triumph Over Satan

12. Who are *"the rulers and authorities"* in verse 15? (See also Ephesians 6:12.)

_____

_____

13. What are some things Satan is attempting? (See also 2 Corinthians 11:3.)

_____

_____

_____

14. Read 2 Corinthians 5:17-21. What does the fact that Satan has been disarmed do for us?

_____

_____

_____

❖ Colossians 2:16-19—The Problem With Religion

15. A person's behavior is often a good indicator of his or her level of commitment to Christ. Why are the practices listed in verse 16 inadequate and inappropriate?

_____

_____

_____

_____

16. Read Romans 14. List the principles that should guide us in dealing with Christians who have traditions and convictions that differ from our own.

_____

_____

_____

17. Some people today are becoming involved in angel worship. Read Exodus 20:3-4 and Hebrews 1:4-14. Summarize the biblical teaching about angels given in these verses.

_____

_____

_____

18. What great danger can result from overemphasizing the importance of angels?

_____

_____

19. What is God's desire for you as you take your place and do your part in the body of Christ? (See also Ephesians 4:14-16.)

_____

_____

❖ Colossians 2:20-23—The Problem With Worldly Principles

20. How would you put verse 20 into your own words?

_____

_____

21. What are the weaknesses of worldly rules?

_____

_____

Apply what you have learned. The main error Paul was addressing in this 1st-century church was confusion and false teaching regarding the real nature of Jesus. Paul says that *"the whole fullness of deity dwells bodily"* in Christ (Colossians 2:9). What groups of people do you know of today who do not believe this truth? What individuals do you know who don't recognize the true nature of Jesus? Will you pray for these groups and individuals? Perhaps God will give you an opportunity to dialogue with them about who Jesus really is. Are you ready?

Christ's Supremacy
Colossians 2:8-23

The Problem With Reason

It was unthinkable to Paul that people whom Christ had set free would allow themselves to be taken captive by false philosophies and human traditions. Human traditions are deceptive because they change with the whims of culture and times; they have no absolutes to guide them.

Few people still believe that right and wrong have clear meanings, or that there is universal truth. But biblical truth does not change. It is the only dependable source of information about God and salvation.

The Christian faith is based on historical fact and direct revelation from God. The Christian faith has an objective basis. Paul presents us with the truth that Christ is God in human form: *"In Him the whole fullness of deity dwells bodily"* (2:9). The Bible has no clearer statement of Christ's deity.

If Jesus is who He claimed to be—*the* way, *the* truth, and *the* life—then it is also true that *"no one comes to the Father"* but by Him (John 14:6). All His claims of uniqueness and the right to be worshiped and obeyed are true and indisputable (Jeremiah 10:10-15). If our knowledge of God is primarily to be found in Christ, then what He says about right and wrong, about salvation and damnation, is crucial.

In Colossians 2:11-12 circumcision and baptism are linked, suggesting that just as circumcision was the outward sign of identification with Israel's corporate life and covenant relationship with God, water baptism is the outward sign of identification with the corporate life of Christ's people in the church and of our covenant relationship with Christ. While speaking about baptism, Paul sets forth three essential truths in verse 12: (1) We have been buried with Christ in baptism, an act symbolic of death to a former self-centered life with its evil deeds, and resurrection to a new Christ-centered life of purity; (2) We have been raised to live a resurrected life because of our faith in God's power; and (3) God raised Jesus from the dead.

The Power of Revelation

Look at what Christ has done. He made us alive, He forgave all our sins, and He canceled the legal code. The legal code is so impossible to keep that everyone falls short of God's standards. But He canceled it, took it away by *"nailing it to the cross"* (2:14).

When the Romans crucified a man, they nailed on the cross over his head a sign stating the crime for which he was executed. Paul tells us that when Jesus died to pay for our sins, a list of our sins was figuratively nailed to the cross—because it was our sin that sent Christ to His death. When Jesus said, *"It is finished"* (John 19:30), He was pronouncing forgiveness and pardon. For everyone who would ask for the payment He made to be applied to *their* list, it would be marked, "Paid in full."

Think about why God raised Christ from the dead and declared His sacrifice adequate to pay for all our sin. Christ Jesus, the Lord of Glory, gave His life on the Cross so that your sin-stained record could be cleansed and you could enjoy His forgiveness and love for eternity. Don't make the mistake, however, of assuming that your relationship with God is automatically assured because God loves you and Jesus died for you. He has done His part, but you must do yours also. You must ask for forgiveness in order to experience the benefit of what He did.

The Problem With Religion

Human beings have two basic heart needs: to remove the guilt of the past and to be assured of a bright eternal future. All religious movements attempt to answer these basic needs. Legalism and the overemphasis of religious experiences are two inadequate ways the Christian community has sometimes addressed these needs.

Asceticism (legalism) was an issue in Colossae as well. Asceticism emphasizes prohibitions and regulations, things a religious person may *not* do and the things a religious person *must* do. Although the moral law still had value for Colossians, the strict insistence on observing various festivals and dietary restrictions was causing the most important thing— the worship of Christ—to be lost.

Paul insists that the Colossians'attempts to please God and mature in faith by keeping a set of prohibitions do not work. Human commands, worldly wisdom, and false humility will have no lasting effect, for they are only man's temporary efforts to be godly. Asceticism lacks the ability to restrain sinful passions, and may produce pride because it addresses outward behavior without dealing with hidden attitudes.

Overemphasis of religious experiences involving angels and visions was another issue in Colossae. While experiences may sometimes be part of the Christian experience, they are not the basis for faith, and if not handled carefully, can cause a person to become *"puffed up without reason by his sensuous mind and not holding fast to the Head* [Christ]*"* (2:18-19). Regarding angel worship, this aberration of the worship of God originated with the early Gnostics, who believed that because God is holy, He could have no close contact with this sinful world. So they believed He needed angelic intermediaries. Paul warns against the error of overemphasis on either legalism or mysticism—performance or experience.

Colossians 2:19 is a warning to anyone who is tempted to follow leaders who claim that God has given a special vision to them alone. If a teacher comes along with a "new" message or forces practices unsupported by the Christian church over the past 2,000 years, it may be a signal that the teacher is not connected with Jesus, the Head of the church. Cults are born in such an environment. If the church is rightly connected to Christ, the Head, its basic doctrine and practice will not depart from the clear teaching of Scripture.

Personalize this lesson.

 The Colossians aren't the only ones who got confused about what following Jesus really means. They were tempted to turn the Christian life into a system of rules to follow, religious days to observe, and certain experiences to have. But we are no less susceptible to these pitfalls today. How are religious practices, observances, and experiences different from *"holding fast to the Head, from whom the whole body … grows"* (2:19)? Is your focus in the right place? If not, tell Jesus what you'd like His help in changing so that you can be truly connected with Him and living through Him.

Christ's Love
Colossians 3:1-17

Memorize God's Word: Colossians 2:6-7.

❖ Colossians 3:1-4—Affections and Ambitions

1. What are the two things we are commanded to do in verses 1-2?

   _____

   _____

   _____

2. Why are we to refocus our affections away from earthly things?

   _____

   _____

   _____

3. What do you think it means to *"appear with* [Christ] *in glory"*? (See also 1 John 3:2.)

   _____

   _____

   _____

❖ Colossians 3:5-9a—Dealing With Sins

4.   a.   In the columns below, write the sins Paul lists, thinking as you do so of how each affects you individually or our society as a whole.

List 1: Verse 5	List 2: Verses 8-9

      b.   How would you categorize the two lists? _____

_____

_____

_____

5.   What does Paul say is coming *"on account of these"*?

_____

_____

❖ Colossians 3:9b-11—Changed by Christ's Love

6.   What are we to put off and put on according to verses 9 and 10?

_____

_____

_____

7.   Reread Colossians 1:9-12; 2:2-3; and 3:9-10. How does knowledge help us battle against the sins mentioned in verses 8 and 9?

_____

_____

_____

_____

8. How have distinctions between classes of people been erased, according to verse 11?

_____

_____

9. Why is prejudice thoroughly inappropriate in the life of a Christian?

_____

_____

_____

❖ Colossians 3:12-14—Clothed in Christ's Love

10. What motivation for being loving to others is given in verse 12?

_____

_____

_____

11. What virtues are we to clothe ourselves with?

_____

_____

_____

12. If you indulged in the vices listed in verses 8-9, what do you think the result would be?

_____

_____

_____

13. Conversely, what would almost certainly be the result of the virtues listed in verses 12-13?

_____

_____

_____

❖ Colossians 3:15-17—Content in Christ's Love

14. What commands are given in these three verses?

_____

_____

_____

15. How are *peace* and *thanksgiving* related to one another?

_____

_____

_____

16. What is the evidence that Christ's Word dwells *"richly"* in you or in someone else?

_____

_____

_____

Apply what you have learned. When you welcome Christ into your life, God immediately declares you to be a new creature in Christ. But although you have *"put on the new self,"* a lot of the old self clings like a polyester shirt full of static electricity. It almost has to be peeled off, and sometimes sparks fly. Getting rid of the old self and embracing the new is a process of *becoming* what God has declared you to be. It's not easy, but it is a great privilege to be clothed in the attributes of Christ. By engaging in Bible study, you have already started the process. Spending time reflecting on God's Word, making sure to put it into practice, is a great way to speed the process of "changing your clothes."

Christ's Love
Colossians 3:1-17

Affections and Ambitions

"If then you have been raised with Christ, seek the things that are above, where Christ is" (3:1). When we become Christians, God asks us to put away the old life and fully embrace our new identity. Verses 3-4 say, *"For you have died, and your life is hidden with Christ in God. When Christ who is your life appears, then you also will appear with Him in glory."* With such glory in the future, there should be joy in the present. We are destined to live with Christ forever in glory. That assurance gives birth to a desire to live for Him now.

Think about what interferes with our relationships. More marriages are torn apart by neglect than by overt betrayal. Similarly, if we get entangled in the things of this world, our affections are misdirected and the spiritual damage can drive a wedge between us and the Lord. We need to *"set* [our] *minds on things above"* (Colossians 3:2). Remembering that He loved us enough to die for us should cause loving gratitude to well up in our hearts so that we find the time to be with Him and to nurture our relationship. We will be with Him forever—but we can start enjoying time with Him *now*.

Enemies of Christ's Love

Colossians 3 was written to a society with social issues much like our own. They, too, engaged in sex without restraint or regard for personhood. They, too, exploited the helpless. And, like us, they had little opposition from society as a whole. Into this culture so much like ours came the gospel of Jesus Christ. It created a new society. It offered an alternative to exploitation, greed, unbridled passion, and perversion for profit. It lifted people out of the gutter and gave them dignity as children of God.

Many people today reject Christ's claims but are still drawn to the kind of world that the gospel produces. They want others to adopt Christian principles and halt society's moral drift, but they have no intention of allowing God to come too close to their own hearts and lives. But Paul ties belief and conduct together. Without a personal commitment to Christ, it is impossible to adopt and apply the basic standards Scripture teaches. Society's decay and disintegration is the observable result of separating belief from conduct.

Paul lists some of the more obvious sins that are troublesome enemies of Christ's love:

- ❖ Sexual immorality: anything working against the lifelong union of a man and a woman in the safety of the marriage bond
- ❖ Passion: inordinate lust or uncontrolled desire
- ❖ Impurity: anything that pollutes the life or character of an individual or society
- ❖ Evil desire: perversion, the distortion or degradation of a good impulse or passion
- ❖ Covetousness: selfish indulgence at the expense of others, the opposite of the desire to give

The logic of this chapter leads to the conclusion that greed is a form of idolatry. Since we have been raised with Christ, who died for our salvation, to put anything ahead of our desire for Him and His generosity is greedy and idolatrous. Doing so will affect our relationship with God and with people. Lust degrades people and causes society to disintegrate. But verse 6 gives us a more important reason: Sin makes God angry! *"On account of these, the wrath of God is coming."*

Paul goes on to list the enemies of Christ's love:

- ❖ Anger: hatred, a chronic bad attitude
- ❖ Wrath: passionate outbursts of anger, rage
- ❖ Malice: a desire to harm, to wish evil on others
- ❖ Slander: to defame the character of another
- ❖ Obscene talk: filthy and abusive talk

Believers lack integrity when they claim to be followers of Christ but live sinful lives, inconsistent with Christ's nature. We are called to allow Christ's love to change us as we are *"renewed in knowledge after the image of [our] Creator"* (3:10).

Effects of Christ's Love

Verse 12 is a call to dress up because we are going to see the King.

Consider the clothes fitting for those who represent God:

- ❖ Compassionate hearts: includes all the values that motivate us to act in a caring way.
- ❖ Kindness: means helping someone carry their load. It is not just feeling sympathy for people in need—it is taking action to help them.
- ❖ Humility: Christ is the greatest example. Philippians 2 tells us that even though He is God, He willingly came to earth, took on the form of a servant, and became obedient even unto death.
- ❖ Meekness: contrasts with wrath (verse 5). Humility and gentleness are not signs of weakness; both illustrate strength under control.
- ❖ Patience: a quality that endures without demanding vengeance. Patience continues working through a problem until an appropriate end is achieved.

"Forgiving each other as the Lord has forgiven you" (3:13) challenges us to adopt the same commitment, integrity, patience, gentleness, and humility that Christ exhibited on the cross when He prayed, *"Father, forgive them, for they know not what they do"* (Luke 23:34).

"And above all these put on love, which binds everything together in perfect harmony" (Colossians 3:14). Christian love is a deliberate decision to act lovingly. It is the virtue that brings unity to the church. Verses 15-17 advise us to let our lives be controlled by the peace of Christ and the Word of Christ. These characteristics are evidence of the Holy Spirit's presence in our lives, for the Spirit prompts us to love God's Word, teach and admonish with wisdom, sing praises to the Lord, have thankful hearts, and give honor to Jesus for every good thing we do, rather than crediting ourselves.

Paul closes this section by reminding the Colossians (and us): *"Whatever you do, in word or deed, do everything in the name of the Lord Jesus, giving thanks to God the Father through Him"* (3:17).

Personalize this lesson.

☑ Think about "putting on" love in the same way you get dressed every morning. How can this illustration change the way you see yourself and your opportunities to be an agent of harmony? What are some ways you can "wear" love as you go into the situations this next week brings?

Christ's Lordship
Colossians 3:18-4:18

Memorize God's Word: Colossians 2:9-10.

❖ Colossians 3:18—A Word to Wives

1. How would you state the command to wives in your own words?
    (See also Ephesians 5:21-24.)

    _____

    _____

2. From both verse 18 and Ephesians 5:21-24, what would you say
    are some of the reasons for this instruction?

    _____

    _____

    _____

3. Describe how Christ was submissive to the Father. (See
    1 Corinthians 11:3; Philippians 2:1-8.)

    _____

    _____

    _____

4. Did Christ's submission affect His worth as a person or imply
    inferiority? (Review Colossians 1:19; 2:9.)

    _____

    _____

5. Read Acts 5:29. What moral limits are implied in the husband and wife relationship?

_____

_____

❖ Colossians 3:19—A Word to Husbands

6. How would you state the command to husbands in your own words?

_____

_____

7. Read Ephesians 5:25-30. What illustration is used to show husbands the logic for loving their wives, and the perfect example of love?

_____

_____

8. How does Christ treat us even when we disappoint or disobey Him (Ephesians 4:29-5:2)?

_____

_____

9. What impact should a godly husband have on his wife's character and personality (Ephesians 5:25-27)?

_____

_____

❖ Colossians 3:20-21—A Word to Children and Fathers/Parents

10. Read Proverbs 1:8-9. Many parents today must play dual roles; these verses can apply to all parents. Why do you think God requires children to obey their parents?

_____

_____

11. Read Exodus 20:12. What do you think it means to *"honor"* your parents?

_____

_____

12. What does God promise as a reward for honoring one's parents, according to Deuteronomy 5:16?

_____

_____

13. From Colossians 3:21, what results when fathers (parents) are overbearing?

_____

_____

14. What instructions does Ephesians 6:4 give to fathers?

_____

_____

❖ Colossians 3:22-4:1—A Word to Workers and "Masters"

15. What is the Christian work ethic described in verses 22-24?

_____

_____

16. What should motivate a Christian to work earnestly and honestly?

_____

_____

17. What is an employer's obligation to workers?

_____

_____

18. What is the motivation to treat employees fairly?

_____

_____

❖ Colossians 4:2-18—Partners in Ministry

19. What should characterize our interactions with non-Christians, according to verses 5 and 6?

_____

_____

20. Read Matthew 5:13.

   a. Record your thoughts about the importance and uses of salt.

_____

_____

_____

   b. What insight does this give you about the spiritual dimension of *being* salt?

_____

_____

_____

Apply what you have learned. The world's ways often conflict with what the Bible teaches, and "swimming against the tide" of public opinion is never easy. What is one area in which this lesson hits home for you personally? Ask God for wisdom and courage to apply what you studied this week to the roles in which you serve.

Christ's Lordship
Colossians 3:18-4:18

Sincere Hearts

Paul insists that God expects exemplary behavior from us. Prevailing 1st-century attitudes must have made that seem incredibly impractical. In Jewish society, the law considered a woman to be the possession of her father or husband. She had no legal rights. Her husband could divorce her for any cause he considered appropriate. She could not divorce him unless he became a leper, turned against the faith as an apostate, or was convicted of raping a virgin.

In this staunchly patriarchal culture, all the privileges belonged to the husbands and all the obligations to the wives. But into its unbalanced social structure comes the liberating, equalizing gospel with its balance of obligations and privileges. *"Here there is not Greek and Jew, circumcised and uncircumcised, barbarian, Scythian, slave, free; but Christ is all, and in all"* (Colossians 3:11). The social barriers are broken down and all believers are seen as brothers and sisters in Christ, fellow heirs of the grace of life. Each has privileges and duties that restore dignity to every person regardless of class, race, gender, or age.

What can ensure love, dignity, freedom, and joy within the bond of marriage? A balance between privilege and obligation. Paul begins by discussing the wife's role. The word *submit* is offensive to many people. Therefore, before going too deeply into the specifics, we need to understand certain underlying assumptions:

  ❖   The setting is one of equality in Christ.
  ❖   Submission is to a specific man—the husband—not to men in general.
  ❖   The relationship between Christ and the Father is the example of submission that wives and husbands are called to follow.

Does Christ's submissive relationship with the Father diminish, stifle, or demean Him in any way? Obviously not. There is no way in which Christ is less than God, nor is His identity threatened by His voluntary submission to the Father. Now consider the marriage relationship in this light. Husbands and wives are equal before God. They have different roles and responsibilities, but this does not make either inferior.

Submission is never a question of value or worth. It is, simply stated, one equal voluntarily submitting to another equal for God's glory. The wife, out of respect for the leadership role God has given to the husband, submits as a voluntary act of obedience to God's command. The husband is to care for his wife as his own body, so her submission to him should not demean or damage her.

Fathers and Children

Because of their lack of knowledge, experience, and the wisdom that normally follows, children are given only one rule—obey your parents. The parallel passage in Ephesians 5:21-24 adds some insight about how the Bible defines godly leadership. Paul gives three qualifiers to shape the command for children to obey their parents:

❖ *in everything* (Colossians 3:20). A child's attitude should be one of obedience rather than rebellion against authority. From the context of this verse, we assume that the parents are Christians seeking to do what is right in the eyes of the Lord.

❖ *in the Lord* (Ephesians 6:1). When parents are obeyed, the Lord is being obeyed, for they govern for Him. When children mature into independent adults, then they assume the responsibility for their own actions and character.

❖ *in honor* (Ephesians 6:2). Honor means that the child respects the parents even when they hold different opinions. *"This pleases the Lord"* (Colossians 3:20). Obedience has no higher motivation.

We can embitter or discourage our children by being inconsistent or inconsiderate, and by placing unrealistic demands on them. A child who lives in a performance-based environment is easily exasperated, and rebellion is the most natural result. Those in authority must be careful to govern in a way that encourages compliance, not rebellion.

Employers and Employees

As Paul moves his focus out of the home and into the workplace, he ignores the question of slavery as an institution and addresses the quality of service instead. People can find themselves bound by an attitude of drudgery toward their work. At the other extreme, they may be workaholics, always putting their jobs before other priorities. Faithfulness to Christ—not just to the boss —is the correct attitude to motivate Christians. Ephesians 6:7 says to serve *"with a good will as to the Lord and not to man."* Showing obedience and respect to those in authority over us as we work shows our obedience and respect for Christ.

Think about husbands and wives, parents and children, employers and employees—God Himself has laid out a plan in relationships that could transform the homes and workplaces of our nation. Relationships work when everyone recognizes we have *"a Master in heaven"* (4:1), and we live, love, work, and play by His rules. But not everyone knows and not everyone plays fair. Does that excuse us from our responsibility to obey when we do know Him and His rules?

Final Instructions

Paul exhorts the church to become a praying church. Paul reminds the Colossians that their attitude should be watchful and thankful. Then he asks for prayer for himself, specifically that he might have opportunities to *"declare the mystery of Christ"* (4:3) and the ability to proclaim it effectively. He also encourages them to be prepared to make the most of the opportunities they have. The ordinary Christian is to be wise about how he acts toward unbelievers and to be careful that his conversation is balanced—both gracious and convicting.

Final Greetings

Paul closes his letter with personal greetings to a special few from him and his co-workers. The people he greets and the ones who send greetings share common ground, for Christ has transformed all of them. Some have been called to leave family and friends and live a traveling lifestyle. Others have been prompted to stay home and use their resources to build up the local church. Each one knows beyond a shadow of a doubt that Jesus is the image of the invisible God, the Creator of everything that exists—and each one has been filled with grace and power because of Him.

Personalize this lesson.

How is your relationship with your spouse, children, parents, employer, or employees? What challenges you as you think about the type of relationships God wants you to have? Are there changes you'd like to pray about and ask Him to help you make?

In what ways has God challenged and encouraged through your study of Colossians? Talk to God or a friend—or both!—about one or two of these. Ask God to help you to pray about and incorporate them into your life.

Small Group Leader's Guide

While *Engaging God's Word* is great for personal study, it is generally even more effective and enjoyable when studied with others. Studying with others provides different perspectives and insights, care, prayer support, and fellowship that studying on your own does not. Depending on your personal circumstances, consider studying with your family or spouse, with a friend, in a Sunday school, with a small group at church, work, or in your neighborhood, or in a mentoring relationship.

In a traditional Community Bible Study class, your study would involve a proven four-step method: personal study, a small group discussion facilitated by a trained leader, a lecture covering the passage of Scripture, and a written commentary about the same passage. *Engaging God's Word* provides two of these four steps with the study questions and commentary. When you study with a group, you add another of these— the group discussion. And if you enjoy teaching, you could even provide a modified form of the fourth, the lecture, which in a small group setting might be better termed a wrap-up talk.

Here are some suggestions to help leaders facilitate a successful group study.

1. Decide how long you would like each group meeting to last. For a very basic study, without teaching, time for fellowship, or group prayer, plan on one hour. If you want to allow for fellowship before the meeting starts, add at least 15 minutes. If you plan to give a short teaching, add 15 or 20 minutes. If you also want time for group prayer, add another 10 or 15 minutes. Depending on the components you include for your group, each session will generally last between one and two hours.

2. Set a regular time and place to meet. Meeting in a church classroom or a conference room at work is fine. Meeting in a home is also a good option, and sometimes more relaxed and comfortable.

3. Publicize the study and/or personally invite people to join you.

4. Begin praying for those who have committed to come. Continue to pray for them individually throughout the course of the study.

5. Make sure everyone has his or her own book at least a week before you meet for the first time.

6. Encourage group members to read the first lesson and do the questions before they come to the group meeting.

7. Prepare your own lesson.

8. Prepare your wrap-up talk, if you plan to give one. Here is a simple process for developing a wrap-up talk:

    a. Divide the passage you are studying into two or three divisions. Jot down the verses for each division and describe the content of each with one complete sentence that answers the question, "What is the passage about?"

    b. Decide on the central idea of your wrap-up talk. The central idea is the life-changing principle found in the passage that you believe God wants to implant in the hearts and minds of your group. The central idea answers the question, "What does God want us to learn from this passage?"

    c. Provide one illustration that would make your central idea clear and meaningful to your group. This could be an illustration from your own life, or a story you've read or heard somewhere else.

    d. Suggest one application that would help your group put the central idea into practice.

    e. Choose an aim for your wrap-up talk. The aim answers the question, "What does God want us to do about it?" It encourages specific change in your group's lives, if they choose to respond to the central idea of the passage. Often it takes the form of a question you will ask your group: "Will you, will I choose to … ?"

9. Show up early to the study so you can arrange the room, set up the refreshments (if you are serving any), and welcome people as they arrive.

10. Whether your meeting includes a fellowship time or not, begin the discussion time promptly each week. People appreciate it when you respect their time. Transition into the discussion with prayer, inviting God to guide the discussion time and minister personally to each person present.

11. Model enthusiasm to the group. Let them know how excited you are about what you are learning—and your eagerness to hear what God is teaching them.

12. As you lead through the questions, encourage everyone to participate, but don't force anyone. If one or two people tend to dominate the discussion, encourage quieter ones to participate by saying something like, "Let's hear from someone who hasn't shared yet." Resist the urge to teach during discussion time. This time is for your group to share what they have been discovering.

13. Try to allow time after the questions have been discussed to talk about the "Apply what you have learned," "Think about" and "Personalize this lesson" sections. Encourage your group members in their efforts to partner with God in allowing Him to transform their lives.

14. Transition into the wrap-up talk, if you are doing one (see number 8).

15. Close in prayer. If you have structured your group to allow time for prayer, invite group members to pray for themselves and one another, especially focusing on the areas of growth they would like to see in their lives as a result of their study. If you have not allowed time for group prayer, you as leader can close this time.

16. Before your group finishes their final lesson, start praying and planning for what your next *Engaging God's Word* study will be.

About Community Bible Study

For almost 40 years Community Bible Study has taught the Word of God through in-depth, community-based Bible studies. With nearly 700 classes in the United States as well as classes in more than 70 countries, Community Bible Study purposes to be an "every-person's Bible study, available to all."

Classes for men, women, youth, children, and even babies, are all designed to make members feel loved, cared for, and accepted— regardless of age, ethnicity, socio-economic status, education, or church membership. Because Bible study is most effective in one's heart language, Community Bible Study curriculum has been translated into more than 50 languages.

Community Bible Study makes every effort to stand in the center of the mainstream of historic Christianity, concentrating on the essentials of the Christian faith rather than denominational distinctives. Community Bible Study respects different theological views, preferring to focus on helping people to know God through His Word, grow deeper in their relationships with Jesus, and be transformed into His likeness.

Community Bible Study's focus ... is to glorify God by providing in-depth Bible studies and curriculum in a Christ-centered, grace-filled, and philosophically safe environment.

Community Bible Study's passion ... is the transformation of individuals, families, communities, and generations through the power of God's Word, making disciples of the Lord Jesus Christ.

Community Bible Study's relationship with local churches ... is one of support and respect. Community Bible Study classes are composed of people from many different churches; they are designed to complement and not compete with the ministry of the local church. Recognizing that the Lord has chosen the local church as His primary channel of ministry, Community Bible Study encourages class members to belong to and actively support their local churches and to be servants and leaders in their congregations.

Do you want to experience lasting transformation in your life? Are you ready to go deeper in God's Word? There is probably a Community Bible Study near you! Find out by visiting www.findmyclass.org or scan the QR code on this page.

For more information:

Call   800-826-4181

Email   info@communitybiblestudy.org

Web   www.communitybiblestudy.org

Class   www.findmyclass.org

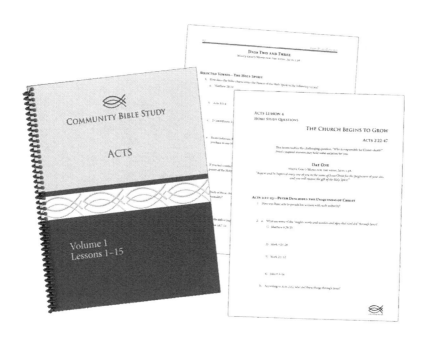

Where will your next Bible study adventure take you?

Engage Bible Studies help you discover the joy and the richness of God's Word and apply it your life.

Check out these titles for your next adventure:

Engaging God's Word: Genesis

Engaging God's Word: Deuteronomy

Engaging God's Word: Joshua & Judges

Engaging God's Word: Daniel

Engaging God's Word: Job

Engaging God's Word: Mark

Engaging God's Word: Luke

Engaging God's Word: Acts

Engaging God's Word: Romans

Engaging God's Word: Galatians

Engaging God's Word: Ephesians

Engaging God's Word: Philippians

Engaging God's Word: Colossians

Engaging God's Word: 1 & 2 Thessalonians

Engaging God's Word: Hebrews

Engaging God's Word: James

Engaging God's Word: 1 & 2 Peter

Engaging God's Word: Revelation

Available at Amazon.com and in fine bookstores.

Visit engagebiblestudies.com

Made in United States
Orlando, FL
07 September 2023

36799204R00035